Jackie Robinson
Breaking Barriers

Victor Crisp

INFOMAX COMMON CORE READERS

Rosen Classroom™

New York

Published in 2014 by The Rosen Publishing Group, Inc.
29 East 21st Street, New York, NY 10010

Book Design: Katelyn Londino

Photo Credits: Cover Photo File/Hulton Archive/Getty Images; pp. 3–24 (both backgrounds) David Lee/Shutterstock.com; p. 5 Hulton Archive/Archive Photos/Getty Images; p. 7 (Robinson family) Hulton Archive/Getty Images; p. 7 (map) Globe Turner/Shutterstock.com; p. 9 Archive Photos/Moviepix/Getty Images; p. 11 Murray Garrett/Archive Photos/Getty Images; pp. 13, 21 Transcendental Graphics/Getty Images Sport/Getty Images; p. 15 en.wikipedia.org/wiki/File:Jrobinson.jpg/Wikipedia.org; p. 17 Mark Kauffman/Sports Illustrated/Getty Images; p. 19 Diamond Images/Getty Images.

ISBN: 978-1-4777-2631-0
6-pack ISBN: 978-1-4777-2632-7

Manufactured in the United States of America

CPSIA Compliance Information: Batch #CS13RC: For further information contact Rosen Publishing, New York, New York at 1-800-237-9932.

Contents

Barriers in America

In America's history, there have been times when some people weren't treated equally. Some people were judged by the color of their skin and didn't have the same rights as white citizens. In the 1900s, many African Americans stood up for their rights and accomplished many things.

Jackie Robinson was an African American athlete who broke many of the **barriers** of inequality. He became the first African American to play baseball for a **major league** team.

Today, Jackie Robinson is remembered as a great athlete. He will continue to be an important part of American history for breaking barriers.

Jackie Robinson was born in Cairo, Georgia, in 1919. At this time, the South wasn't a friendly place for African Americans. They didn't have equal rights and couldn't hold the same jobs or go to the same places as white people. Jackie's mom moved her family to California, where she hoped things might be fairer.

As a boy, Jackie realized that when he played sports, he was judged by his skill, not his skin color.

Jackie's family moved to Pasadena, California. Living there was tough because they were the only African American family in the neighborhood.

Jackie
Robinson

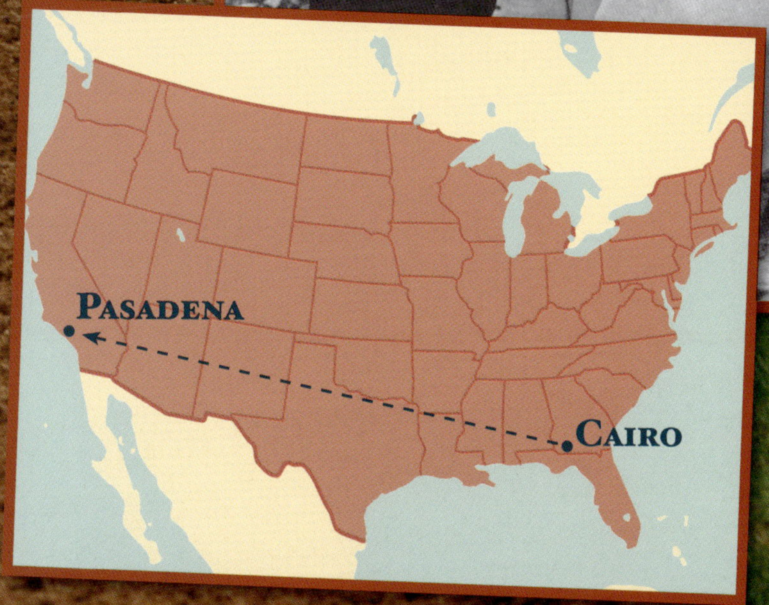
Pasadena
Cairo

Sports Star

Jackie played many different sports. He was chosen as best sports player, or MVP, in the Pasadena area in 1938.

After high school, Jackie went to a college called UCLA to play sports. He was the first person to ever play four sports there at one time! He was a star in basketball, track, baseball, and football. He had to leave UCLA before finishing school because he couldn't afford to go there.

Jackie was a sports star at UCLA, especially in basketball! He was the two-time leader in scoring out of all the major college basketball teams on the West Coast.

18

After UCLA, Jackie moved to Hawaii to play football for the Honolulu Bears. He was soon forced to join the army for World War II. He trained to be an officer, which was a new opportunity for African American men.

However, things still weren't equal in America. African American people were still forced to sit in the back of buses. One time, Jackie wouldn't move to the back of the bus to show how unfair the rules were.

Jackie got in a lot of trouble because he wouldn't go to the back of the bus. He had to leave his job in the army.

A Big Opportunity

Jackie became a **professional** baseball player when he joined the Kansas City Monarchs in 1945. Baseball teams were split into African American teams and white teams. African American teams, such as the Monarchs, weren't in the major leagues.

Jackie was soon noticed for his talent. The Brooklyn Dodgers were a major league team, and their president was a man named Branch Rickey. He thought Jackie should have an opportunity to play in the major leagues.

Branch Rickey knew it wouldn't be easy to hire Jackie for his team. Many people would be angry at him for breaking the rules.

Branch Rickey knew that many people would yell **insults** at Jackie if he joined a major league team. Rickey tested Jackie to make sure he wouldn't be hurt or angry if people insulted him. Jackie passed the test, and Rickey told the public that Jackie would now be playing for the Dodgers.

Jackie's first game with the Dodgers was on April 15, 1947. It was an important moment for African Americans everywhere.

Jackie broke the barrier between white people and African Americans in America's national sport.

B
odgers
42

Branch Rickey was right—people were mean to Jackie. One time, the crowd was so mean that the Dodgers' captain, Pee Wee Reese, decided to do something about it. He walked over to Jackie and put his arm around him. That showed everyone that the Dodgers accepted an African American as a teammate.

Jackie helped the Dodgers win many **championship** games. In his first year, he was voted the best new player!

The World Series is the biggest baseball championship in the United States. The Dodgers won the World Series in 1955 with Jackie's help!

SHELTER
Dodgers
22

Leaving Baseball

In sports, players can be traded to other teams. After almost 10 years of playing for the Dodgers, Jackie was traded to a team called the Brooklyn Giants in 1956. But he decided to stop playing professional baseball, or retire.

In 1962, Jackie was admitted into the Baseball Hall of Fame, which was a great honor. This honor is given only to baseball players who will be remembered for their greatness.

Here, Jackie Robinson holds his Baseball Hall of Fame award. It meant that he was one of the greatest athletes in America!

JACK ROOSEVELT ROBINSON
WILLIAM BOYD McKECHNIE

Even after playing baseball, Jackie still accomplished many things. He was the vice president of a food-service chain called Chock Full o' Nuts. He also had a wife and three children. He continued to speak out for equality for all people.

Jackie died on October 24, 1972. A year later, his wife founded the Jackie Robinson **Foundation** to give students a chance to succeed and to keep his memory alive.

Jackie Robinson went down in history as a man who broke barriers in baseball and in American life.

A Great Athlete

- **1919** — Jackie is born.
- **1938** — Jackie is named MVP in the Pasadena area.
- **1939** — Jackie goes to UCLA.
- **1941** — Jackie plays football for the Honolulu Bears.
- **1945** — Jackie joins the Kansas City Monarchs.
- **1947** — Jackie starts playing for the Brooklyn Dodgers.
- **1956** — Jackie retires from the Dodgers.
- **1962** — Jackie is accepted into the Baseball Hall of Fame.
- **1972** — Jackie dies.

Glossary

barrier (BEHR-ee-uhr) Something that gets in the way of action or progress.

championship (CHAM-pee-uhn-ship) A contest that decides who is the winner of something.

foundation (fown-DAY-shun) A group of people who work for a common purpose and give money to individuals or groups.

insult (IHN-suhlt) Something said or done to hurt another person's feelings.

major league (MAY-juhr LEEG) The highest-level baseball teams in the United States.

professional (pruh-FEH-shuh-nuhl) A person who earns a living by doing a certain job, sport, or art.

Index